*H*umility
Wellspring of Virtue

Other books by Dietrich von Hildebrand
available from Sophia Institute Press:

Confidence in God
The New Tower of Babel
Making Christ's Peace a Part of Your Life
Love, Marriage, and the Catholic Conscience
Marriage: The Mystery of Faithful Love
Transformation in Christ

Humility
Wellspring of Virtue

by Dietrich von Hildebrand

SOPHIA INSTITUTE PRESS®
Manchester, New Hampshire

Sophia Institute Press®
Box 5284, Manchester, NH 03108
1-800-888-9344
website: http:\\www.sophiainstitute.com

Library of Congress Cataloging-in-Publication Data

Von Hildebrand, Dietrich, 1889-
    Humility : wellspring of virtue / by Dietrich von Hildebrand.
        p.   cm.
    Humility is an excerpt from Transformation in
    Christ, published
      in 1990 by Sophia Institute Press.
    Includes bibliographical references.
    ISBN 0-918477-59-X (pbk. : alk. paper)
    1. Humility – Christianity. I. Von Hildebrand,
    Dietrich, 1899-
        Transformation in Christ. II. Title.
BV4647.H8V66   1997
241'.4 – dc21   97-22606 CIP

99 00 01 02 10 9 8 7 6 5 4 3

Contents

NOTE: The biblical quotations in these pages are based on the Douay-Rheims edition of the Old and New Testaments. Some quotations have been cross-referenced with the differing enumeration in the Revised Standard Version, using the following symbol: (RSV =).

Humility
Wellspring of Virtue

*Everyone that exalteth himself shall
be humbled; and he that humbleth
himself shall be exalted.
Luke 14:11*

1.

Humility is the antithesis of pride

*H*umility, as St. Francis de Sales has said, is the highest of all *human* virtues; for love – the consummation of all virtues, on which "dependeth the whole law and the prophets"[1] – is a *divine* virtue.

What is true of love – that without it, all other virtues and good works are valueless – is again, in another respect, true of humility. For, just as love embodies the life of all virtues and expresses the inmost substance of all holiness, humility is the *precondition* and basic presupposition for the genuineness, the beauty, and the truth of all virtue.

It is *mater* and *caput* ("mother" and "fountainhead") of all specifically human virtues; for, inversely, pride (*superbia*) is not only by itself

---

[1] Matt. 22:40.

our primal sin: it also inwardly contaminates all intrinsically good dispositions and robs every virtue of its value before God. A consideration of pride, therefore, will help us better understand the nature and importance of humility.

Pride is worse than concupiscence

We have two great enemies to combat within us: pride and concupiscence.[2] The two are mostly intertwined in some definite manner. Persons tainted by pride alone are seldom to be met with. It is these two enemies that render us blind to value. But they are not of equal importance: it is not concupiscence but pride that constitutes the primal evil in our souls. Satan's original gesture is the act of absolute pride that rebels against God, the embodiment of all values, in an impotent attempt to appropriate His power and dominion.

[2] Concupiscence, a consequence of Original Sin, refers to the disordered desire for sensual pleasures.

True, in the sinfulness of many men (indeed, of most men) concupiscence plays a more conspicuous part; but, nevertheless, it falls short of being the primal evil. That is why in the Gospels even the sin of impurity, however grave, is less severely judged than that of pride. Christ denounced pride and obduracy in far more incisive terms than the sins of the flesh.

Thus, pride is the deepest root of the malignancy within ourselves, which is entirely consonant with the fact that Adam's sin, too, consisted in an act of disobedience inspired not by concupiscence, which was only to be a consequence of the Fall, but by pride.

Humility conquers pride

The fact alone that pride is the primal source of all moral evil clearly demonstrates the paramount importance of humility. What is most essential in the process of dying to ourselves is the conquest of pride and that liberation from one's self whose name is *humility*.

Humility

On the degree of our humility depends the measure in which we shall achieve freedom to participate in God's life and make it possible for the supernatural life received in holy Baptism to unfold in our souls. "God resisteth the proud and giveth grace to the humble."[3] On the other hand, every virtue and every good deed turns worthless if pride creeps into it – which happens whenever in some fashion we glory in our goodness. This is clearly set forth by the parable of the publican and the Pharisee in the Gospel.[4]

Pride has many forms

There exist formally and materially distinct forms of pride. As humility represents an antithesis to every form of pride, a consideration of the various forms and degrees of pride will help us become aware of the various aspects of

[3] James 4:6.
[4] Luke 18:10-14.

humility, each of which expresses a negation of pride in one or another of its manifestations.

Satanic pride hates goodness

Let us begin this survey of the types of pride with the worst and most characteristic one, which we may call satanic pride. He who is afflicted with this knows one kind of satisfaction only: the glorification of his self. For him, the entire world is devoid of interest except insofar as it offers him an opportunity to experience his own superiority, power, and splendor. Subject to this spasm of the ego, enslaved to his exclusive interest in the excellence of his self as such, he is unable to grasp the inherent beauty and nobility of objective values.

Satanic pride blinds

He is, then, blind to value; but his kind of value-blindness is not that dull insensibility to values which marks the slave of concupiscence. On the contrary, he does in a sense grasp the

metaphysical force that resides in value, the
majestic sovereignty proper to it.

However, he grasps it in a way that implies,
at the same time, its profound misconception.
For – and herein precisely consists his value-
blindness – while he is aware of that character
of compelling sovereignty inherent in values,
he fails to see its essential nexus with their self-
contained beauty, their objective significance
independent of any utilitarian or decorative use
in the service of an ego.

Hence, it happens that his value-blindness
bears a tinge, not of dull indifference, but of
hostility. Values, to him, are a scandal; he fatally
endeavors to alienate their sovereignty and trans-
fer it to his own self. He fears them as a menace
to his supreme glory derived from his autono-
mous selfhood; the claim to submission which
emanates from them he meets with resentment and rebellion. He does not, as does the
concupiscent man, content himself with ignor-
ing values and turning a deaf ear to their call.

He would, as it were, *dethrone* them; again and again he performs the impotent gesture which is aimed at depriving them of their metaphysical power.

Frequently enough his endeavor takes the form of an attempt at enthroning some false value in the place of the true ones. In certain typical cases, it is this mechanism of disguised pride which underlies the cult of idols.

This attitude appears most clearly in the rebellion of Lucifer, who would fain be "like God."[5] He shuts his eyes to the goodness and holiness of God; he fails to perceive the indissoluble union between all-powerfulness and all-goodness; he would separate omnipotence from all-goodness and attribute the former to himself. All his thoughts are centered in the one overwhelming consciousness of "counting for much."

This yearning for self-supremacy is not satisfied by terrestrial power, by actual physical power

[5] Gen. 3:5.

as such; he also hungers for the possession of that metaphysical grandeur which is implicit in all possession of value.

Yet, to be sure, it is not for the sake of the value as value that he covets it; what preoccupies him is that mysterious power without which he may not attain the plenitude of power, and which therefore irritates him as an irksome limitation imposed on his pleasure in counting for much.

Thus original pride engenders a hatred of values, a combative opposition to whatever irradiates light, to all self-contained glory – ultimately, to God. Clearly, this attitude is tantamount to ethical evil in an eminent sense; it constitutes the utmost antithesis to the harmony of values and the extreme negation by a creature of his creaturely status. It represents the most express refusal to honor value by an adequate response to its appeal.

Satanic pride isolates and divides

By taking this position, man cuts himself off from the world of values in its entirety. He will be incapable of all response to value, not so much owing to his value-blindness as because he lacks the readiness for submission that underlies all response to value. His value-blindness will be the consequence, not the cause, of his pride. It is, therefore, a blindness that involves a high degree of guilt. Also, pride determines a specifically grave form of obduracy. Its effects diametrically oppose those of love (which opens and melts the soul) and contrast dramatically to the specific qualities of responsive kindness and luminous harmony which love connotes. The proud personality is lacerated by a deep disharmony; a corrosive venom pervades his entire life; and all the gratification he derives from whatever flatters his pride is unable to provide him with any genuine inner happiness, any blissful peace.

Satanic pride turns freedom into license

Another formal characteristic of satanic pride consists in the abuse of liberty. The gift of free decision, conferred upon man as a mark of his likeness to God, is granted him by the divine will so as to empower him to respond to values and to surrender to God in a way that carries the full sanction of his personality. Under the sway of pride, that gift is perverted into a stimulus for his orgy of self-glorification and into nourishment for his consciousness of counting for much.

The basic fact of freedom — the dimension of our being where we most possess ourselves and actualize ourselves — disjoined from its ordination to God and from its correlation with the world of values, becomes the source of an illusion of absolute power and of a primary claim to dominion. Freedom is degraded into arbitrary license.

In certain conditions the man governed by pride will commit this or that action, not because it satisfies his cupidity — or even his pride, so far as its material import goes — but as a mere confirmation and exercise of his independence,

a test of the position of power he derives from
his gift of free will. This is the horrible sin of
Kirilov, the lonesome atheist in Dostoyevsky's
Possessed, who, according to a deliberate plan,
shoots himself at a moment convenient for the
purposes of a gang of nihilist scoundrels, not in
order to promote their revolutionary designs,
but just to prove his absolute liberty unrelated
to any concrete aim or value, the meaningless-
ness of death, and the nonexistence of God. Here
is a key to many an evil deed which apparently
lacks motivation, since by virtue of its contents it
cannot possibly offer its perpetrator any subjective satisfaction, not even a wholly illicit one.

Satanic pride refuses all submission as such

Apart from his antagonism toward the
world of values and its serene harmony, the
maniac of pride repudiates all submission as
such; his "I will not serve" is meant to challenge
any kind of authority; he would bow neither to

15

man nor to God. This specific mode of pride, with its quality of supreme malice, may of course appear in various degrees. It may take hold of a person completely, so that he is no longer able to evoke any response to value and becomes a prey to total value-blindness. Lucifer is the prototype of this absolute pride. By analogy, we may class with him Cain,[6] as well as the figure of Rakitin in Dostoyevsky's *The Brothers Karamazov*.

There is also a category of men who are filled with this form of pride in part only. Their pride is similar in nature, but restricted in extension. These would recognize and esteem certain sets of values – such as justice or faithfulness, for instance, and others not explicitly impinging on their ego-worship or their sense of grandeur – but refuse to take cognizance of, and respond to, values like humility, meekness, or mercy. Such men are but partially afflicted with

[6] Gen. 4:3-16.

value-blindness, nor do they lack a *conditional* readiness to submission. What shocks them is not the intrinsic importance of value as such, but only the claim inherent in certain high values which, by virtue of their particular nature, imply a specific negation of pride and invite man to relinquish it altogether. Values of this order, and not the others, evoke such men's antagonism. Of course, whenever men of this type do display a response to values, it always remains a conditional one, and therefore mutilated and impaired in its quality.

Response to value is fundamental to humility

Humility is, first, an antithesis to all metaphysical pride of the kind just described. In the humble man, the basic attitude of responsiveness to value has the whole field; he is not dominated at all by the desire of absolute power or of counting for much. He grasps the objective meaning of values in its independence from the pursuits of the subject, and honors them with an unhampered and adequate response. The readiness to posit that submission and surrender which belongs to every response to value is present in him. He is concerned with the glory, not of his own ego, but of the objectively important, of that which pleases God. The inward nobility of good, its intrinsic beauty, touches his heart and delights him. In his devotion to the good, he participates in the harmony of values; his soul is bright and serene, free from the corrosive poison that eats the heart of the proud.

True, all this he has in common with everyone in whom the fundamental attitude of response to value has acquired prevalence; that is to say, with everyone who has awakened to a life in the light of moral consciousness.

Not humility alone, but also every response to value and every virtue forms an antithesis to metaphysical pride, which is the stem of moral evil. Opposition to this original pride equally underlies justice, veracity, faithfulness, and even purity, although the opposition specific to the latter is directed toward concupiscence. For all these virtues derive from a value-responsive central attitude; they all presuppose awareness of value, and the readiness to surrender to value and to submit to its demands.

Hence, the antithesis to pride in this sense reveals to us only that element of humility which is alive in all virtue, which constitutes an aspect of the value-response pure and simple. It manifests humility insofar as humility is the basis of all virtues. It does not, however, enable us to grasp the nature of humility in its narrower and specific sense. In the latter, more elements are required than have been described above. We shall see this presently, having considered further types of pride.

2.

Humility rejoices in God's sovereignty

*F*rom satanic pride and the hatred of God it implies, we must distinguish a much milder form of pride – associated with a less fearful variety of rebellion against God – which, nevertheless, still shares the metaphysical character of satanic pride.

We find it in persons who are by no means blind to value and are capable of a positive response to it. With them, the desire to count for much plays no decisive part; nor do they exhibit the specific obduracy of the victims of satanic pride. Their life is not spoiled through and through by disharmony; theirs is not the scorching hatred of light as personified by Alberic in Richard Wagner's opera *The Ring of the Nibelungen*.

On the contrary, they are capable of an honest moral effort; in their lives, the problem

of good and evil may rank paramount; they
may well show great receptiveness to all kinds
of beauty. But they shun the encounter with a
personal God; they evade the full avowal of
their creaturely status; they balk at that ultimate
act of subordination which goes far beyond
what is implied in every response to value.

So long as they are only concerned with the
realm of values (which, after all, they may in a
sense face as *equal partners)*, they are ready to
submit to the call of the object. Nay, they would
even surrender to an Impersonal Absolute, to
which they would be as parts to the whole. For,
so long as there is no question of their relation
with an absolute Person, they may still keep a
last remnant of ego-sovereignty; moreover, as
parts of the whole, they may, after a fashion,
rejoice in their identity with the absolute.

It is only in our encounter with a personal
God that we become fully aware of our condition as creatures, and fling from us the last parti-
cle of self-glory. The idealists who cherish ethical

autonomy, the pantheists, the theosophists: these all are bent on escaping from subordination to an almighty Lord and, consequently, from relinquishing a certain minimum sovereignty which flatters their pride.

Humility acknowledges our creaturely status

By contrasting it with this type of pride, we are better able to grasp the specific nature of humility. Humility involves the full knowledge of our status as creatures, a clear consciousness of having received everything we have from God. "Or what hast thou that thou hast not received? And if thou hast received, why dost thou glory, as if thou hadst not received it?"[7]

It is in humility that we attain to an exact consideration of the metaphysical situation of man. Humility presents in specifically sharp relief that general aspect of all Christian morality – the

[7] 1 Cor. 4:7.

unreserved recognition of the metaphysical situation of man, the attitude of throwing all illusions overboard and granting to the whole of reality the response that is due to it. Thus, it has been said justly: "Humility is truth." Correspondingly, the soul of pride is falsehood, for pride means a refusal to realize our metaphysical situation.

True knowledge of our status as creatures, however, implies a confrontation of the creature with its Creator: it is not possible except in reference to a personal God. For awareness of our creaturely status is more than a mere awareness of our debility and limitation. It amounts to experiencing not only our relative imperfection and the restrictions to which we are subject, but the infinite distance between us and absolute Being; it requires a full understanding of the fact that we have received "all that we have and are" – except sin – from God.

So long as he fights shy of a confrontation of the infinite Person with his finite person, so long

as he clings to an atheistic or pantheistic conception of the world, howsoever flexibly formu-
lated, man can never attain to a fully weighted
awareness of his status as a creature. Either he
will confine himself to an awareness of his dependence on his body and on the surrounding
nature, or else he will see himself in terms of
his participation in an absolute Whole. To the
atheist, who knows no absolute being, no more
than an awareness of our relative limitation and
impotence is possible.

Again, in the pantheist's view, we are parts
of the Absolute, be it even so small and unimportant parts as to be negligible when taken
individually.

Here the distance between us and the Absolute is transposed to the level of quantity. We
still imagine ourselves to be of the stuff of the
Absolute, as it were, and sharers in its glory. A
hidden playground is still reserved for the antics
of a certain refined species of pride; the nerve
of pride has not been cut; the idol of self-glory

has not been thoroughly uprooted. This becomes even clearer when we further consider
the distinction between a mere avowal of our
weakness and true humility. It is only the overwhelming contrast between creature and personal Creator that discloses to us, in all its depth,
the principal fact about ourselves: that we receive
all our being *from* God; that He is That Which
Is, whereas we are "as though we *were not*."

Humility joyfully assents to creatureliness

Furthermore, humility also implies blissful
assent to this our creatureliness and *non-being*.
What it demands is not a reluctant or resigned
admission of our nothingness: it is, primarily,
a joyous response to the infinite glory of God,
similar to what is meant by the words of St.
Catherine of Siena: *Che tu sia ed io non sia*
("That Thou shalt be, and that I shall not be").

The humble man does not want to be anything by his own resources; he is free from all

ambition to be something by his own power and to have to recognize no master over himself. He *wills* to receive everything from God alone. The glory of God makes him happy; he is thus so centered in his love of adoration for God that the idea of being something by his own force – aside from its unreality – would not tempt him at all; nor does the concern about keeping his sovereignty intact carry the slightest meaning to him. Such an attitude, however, is only possible in reference to a personal God; moreover, as Pascal says, "not [in reference] to the God of the philosophers, but to the God of Abraham, Isaac, and Jacob"; above all, to the living God, who approaches and addresses us in the Person of Jesus Christ, His only-begotten Son.

Humility delights in the existence and glory of God

In true humility, then, we may discern three elements. First, *awareness of, and responsiveness*

to, the glory of God. God in His infinite holiness
having revealed Himself to our minds, it is for
us to respond with holy joy and loving adoration. Prior to everything else, we must be filled
with the blissful consciousness that the infinitely
perfect Person – God, who is omnipotent, om-
niscient, and all-good – is the Prime Cause of all
being. We must give, in reference to God, the
pure response to value, our joy being elicited
by His glory alone. That is, we must say with
the holy Church, "We thank Thee for Thy great
glory." Touched by the ray of God's supernatural holiness that transcends all our concepts, we
must exclaim with the Psalmist, "For better is one
day in Thy courts above thousands elsewhere."[8]

Even in perceiving a human value, we may
evince this wholly disinterested, pure joy,
which refers to the existence of value as such.
We rejoice in considering that truth exists, that a
certain good and noble person dwells on earth,

[8] Ps. 83:11 (RSV = Ps. 84:10).

that there are such beautiful things as the starred sky or a great work of art.

But what we have now in mind is our joy related to the fact that the absolute Being is infinitely perfect and that this infinitely glorious Being is a Person. What an immense augmentation of the reality of good is implied in this – that the highest good should not be a mute impersonal something, an idea or a principle, but a Person speaking to us: "I am who am";[9] the absolute Person in whom all values converge at their highest, who has created us and keeps us in being, who embraces us and owns us as only a person can.

Humility calls upon us to allow our hearts to be wounded by the glory of God, to fall on our knees in loving adoration, and to deliver ourselves over to God entirely. We must display that pure response in which our center of gravity is thus transferred from ourselves to God, so

[9] Exod. 3:14.

31

that His glory taken in itself, without any reference to His benevolence toward us, becomes for us a source of precious joy: "My God and my all," said St. Francis of Assisi.

Humility acknowledges our debt to God

Yet, no less essential to true humility is a second step: *the confrontation of our own person with the infinite Person,* who is God. In the face of God we become aware of our sinfulness and our weakness. We say with St. Francis, "Who art Thou, and who am I?" We discern our nothingness and our obscurity and join in the words of the Psalmist, "But I am a worm, and no man."[10] We come to understand that we are utterly in the debt of God and completely dependent upon Him. "Know ye that the Lord is God: he made us, and not we ourselves."[11]

[10] Ps. 21:7 (RSV = Ps. 22:6).
[11] Ps. 99:3 (RSV = Ps. 100:3).

In humility, our knowledge of God's glory fills us with hope and joy

As has been shown above, it is only in our confrontation with God that we gain sight of the measure of our debility and our nothingness. However, the knowledge of our relative imperfection and finiteness would by itself suffice to cast us down and to fill us with despair, unless preceded by a contemplation of the glory of God. The revelation of divine glory is the *objective* condition for the realization of that essential postulate of humility: that the knowledge of our nothingness, far from casting us down or even persuading us into a resigned acceptance of our misery, shall evoke in us a blissful assent to our creaturely status.

Again, the *subjective* condition lies in our assumption of that attitude of responsiveness which enables us to understand a value fully and to take joy in that value in itself. If we are immersed in the prideful, value-blind attitude

which seeks satisfaction in the sovereignty of
the ego alone and in impotent resentment, and
which challenges the majesty of objective value,
then the revelation of the glory of God will itself
be of no avail to us.

In place of blissful self-surrender, it will only
provoke on our part Lucifer's proud gesture of
defiance to God. Nay, given this negative attitude
to value as such, it will be true to say that the
greater the glory which confronts us, the deeper
will be the resentment which it arouses.

In other words, a certain state of mind is req-
uisite on our part so that the objective condition
of humility may operate in our soul.

We must possess the fundamental attitude
of respect which renders value visible for us, as
well as the aliveness to values which enables
us to honor their glory – once we are aware
of it – with a response of love and joy. And,
in order that the value-response of loving ven-
eration and pure joy may blossom out in us,
it is not sufficient for us to be rid of proud

contempt and resentment. The craving for self-sovereignty, the desire to preserve a remnant of the ego's impregnability, must dominate us no longer.

On the other hand, even if we did possess this fundamental attitude which is a predisposition of humility, the knowledge of our creatureliness and sinfulness could not but produce a fearsome feeling of despondency along with some form of the consciousness of inferiority – unless we had already found God, and caught the light of His glory.

He who has true humility is not oppressed and cast down by the knowledge that God is everything and he nothing; no, his awareness of the glory of God carries him in a state of bliss over the precipice of his nothingness and his obscurity. He *wills* that God shall be everything and he nothing; past all oppression and despair, he is filled with a holy longing for God. He lifts his hands to God, exclaiming, "One thing I have asked of the Lord, this will I seek after: that I may dwell in the house of the Lord all the days of my life."[12]

Humility experiences dependence on God as being sheltered by Him

He who possesses humility derives from his confrontation with God not only an awareness of his nothingness and obscurity but a keen experience of his *dependence* as well. He realizes the truth that he is wholly at the mercy of the all-powerful Lord of life and death, that whatever thought he might have of escaping or eluding God could not but be a pure illusion. "Whither shall I go from Thy spirit? Or whither shall I flee from Thy face?"[13]

However, for the Christian, this sense of dependence takes on the aspect of being sheltered in God. The thought of his total impotence in relation to God does not arouse depression or

[12] Ps. 26:4 (RSV = Ps. 27:4).
[13] Ps. 138:7 (RSV = Ps. 139:7).

anguish in him; he does not attempt to keep up an illusion of sovereignty and to arrange his life as though he were his own master.

Rather, he flings himself into the arms of the Almighty; he deliberately assents to his status of dependence, and prays with the holy Church, "Into Thy hands, O Lord, I commend my spirit."[14] Humility, then, contains not merely the knowledge of our dependence on God but the active conformity of our will to it; our blissful surrender to God. The humble one feels sheltered in God, indeed, as a possession of God: "We are his people and the sheep of his pasture."[15]

[14] Cf. Ps. 30:6 (RSV = Ps. 31:5).
[15] Ps. 99:3 (RSV = Ps. 100:3).

3.

Humility recognizes man's dignity

*F*or humility demands that we not only take account of the personality of God but at the same time remain fully conscious of our own. Our awareness of "being naught" must not by any means entail on our part a tendency to de-personalization, a kind of a drab submersion in impersonal nature. That blissful assent to our creatureliness and our nothingness, our entire dependence on God, must be given freely and expressly: it must be, precisely, a *personal* act *par excellence*. Humility does not command a rejection of one's own self, pure and simple.

Although we are nothing by ourselves, although *everything* we have is received – still, we have received *a great deal* from God. In the first place, humility certainly is our response to the infinite distance that separates absolute from creaturely being. Secondly, it is a response to the fact that whatever we have, we have received from God rather than brought about by ourselves. We grow aware, in humility, of our impotence and our total dependence on God. Finally, we fathom the depths of our wretchedness, our sinfulness, and our pitifulness; we are struck by the divine plenitude of light and our own obscurity.

Yet, by the same token we also realize what God has granted to us. First of all, humility must not cause us to forget the fact that God has created us in His *likeness,* that we are spiritual persons. It is not lack of humility which makes the Psalmist say: "Thou hast made [man] a little less than the angels."[16] Any form of the negation of our nature as a spiritual person (be it, say, materialism or the worship of vital force) — any idea of leveling down the incomparable ontological superiority of man to all mere vital being, let alone to mere matter — is hopelessly remote

[16] Ps. 8:6 (RSV = Ps. 8:5).

from the attitude of true humility. For a denial of that ontological dignity which God has conferred on us forcibly involves a disregard for the glory and all-powerfulness of God; yet humility is above all *a recognition of the glory of God,* and in a secondary sense only, a recognition of our own unimportance.

Beyond the natural dignity God has conferred on man, Christian humility will recall that far higher and ineffable gift of divine mercy, its call upon man to participate in divine life, and the imparting of supernatural life through Baptism.

Pantheism depersonalizes man

The humble Christian, therefore, will be the last to emulate the pantheist in minimizing human personality or regarding man as a *quantité négligeable.* He will not become a victim of that infatuation for size which, in view of the colossal dimensions of material nature or the immensity of the solar systems, suggests a notion of man as a mere drop in the world's great ocean. If this

43

were so, man's actions could never, of course, mean more than a sequence of irrelevant details in the process of nature. Behind this suicidal nihilism – as we have already hinted – a kind of sinister pride is hidden; for howsoever its teachers may emphasize the irrelevance of man, from their conception of being constituent parts of this vast and divinized cosmos they again snatch a vertiginous sense of bigness; at bottom, that vast cosmos is nothing but an ego inflated beyond measure with which one may identify oneself.

The individual's alleged function of being a *part of the great whole* holds out a compensation for pride; for the significance one may yet have as part of the whole is at any rate inherent in what is ultimately the same thing as oneself, and not a gift from above, from an absolute Being radically different in kind.

Inasmuch as it denies a personal Godhead – creating out of nothing a world distinct from itself, through a free act of its will – pantheism, of necessity, blurs the concept of man as a finite being. A relation between whole and part supersedes the bond between Creator and creature.

This has the double implication, on the one hand, of raising man to the level of absolute being, thus making his finiteness ambiguous; and on the other hand, of depriving him of the character of a distinct being and consequently of his peculiar dignity in contrast to the rest of nature. Regardless of the contradiction implicit in such a conception, an impersonal absolute is posited (although it cannot be but something metaphysically inferior to the persons who are supposed to be parts of it), and man is subordinated to that impersonal absolute. Man, a spiritual person, rests with his being in the nonpersonal absolute that engulfs him – an interpretation that is clearly intended to divest him of his character as a person.

This implies a tragic misconception of man's metaphysical situation. Viewed as a drop in the world's vast ocean, man is cheated of his specific dignity and his central importance. He is thus appreciated far below what is due to him. Again, being made part and parcel of the absolute – although in fact a sham absolute, beneath the level of personality and hence bare of dignity – he is on the other hand enormously overestimated. This is the aspect that panders to his pride.

Further, *the depersonalization of God points unmistakably to a depersonalization of man as well.* By assimilating man – as part of an impersonal deity – to the absolute, we at the same time displace his center of gravity from the sphere of personality within him into the impersonal lower regions of his nature. The rash attempt to elevate him to a level of absoluteness operates, actually, toward his degradation.

Polytheism trivializes God

In ancient *polytheism,* man, it is true, is created by a personal god; but this god, Jupiter, is himself finite. There can be no question, therefore, of a confrontation of man as a finite being with the *absolute,* the uncreated, the infinite. By virtue of the anthropomorphic conception of the gods, the pattern of earthly existence is projected upon the level of eternity; it is not human life which, in the *conspectus* of the absolute, acquires a universal and indelible meaning, but inversely, the world of the gods which becomes tinged with the flighty irrelevance of terrestrial life – hence, the trait of playfulness which, in Homeric antiquity, seems invariably to cling to the image of man, as though he were irrevocably confined in his finiteness.

Here the transcendental glance of man which seeks for something absolute and simple – something that surpasses all manifoldness *per eminentiam* – is directed toward a mere magnified finiteness charged with all the motley plurality of earthly things. Man allows his ties with true Divinity to wither; he casts himself before the idols of which the Psalmist says, "They have eyes and see not: they have ears and hear not . . . they have hands and feel not."[17]

---

[17] Ps. 113:5-7 (RSV = Ps. 115:5-7).

True, man does not fall a victim to depersonalization; but he is deprived of his ordination
to the absolute and the possibility of confrontation with God. This, too, portends a fundamental loss of the deepest significance and nobility
of man, chiefly because it conjures away the
gravity and depth inherent in man's metaphysical situation.

Contrast this with the Old Testament,
which clearly conceives of man as a creature
and person facing his personal Creator in full
distinctness. There man's whole life is dominated by the great dialogue between himself,
the created person, and God, the living, knowing, and loving God, Creator of Heaven and
earth.

Humility allows us to see our true moral and metaphysical condition

He who has the virtue of humility knows
that the infinite love and mercy of God "spared
not even his own Son, but delivered Him up

for us all."[18] He is aware of the importance of
each immortal soul before God: "Precious in
the sight of God is the death of His saints."[19]
Against the background of what he has received
from God, in the light of the gratuitous gifts
of God and the high call addressed to him, he
comes to understand that he is nothing by his
own force, that he has made inadequate use of
the natural endowments as well as of the supernatural gifts of grace he owes to God, that he is
but an "unprofitable servant."[20]

Humility is closely connected with that holy
freedom in which we acquire the proper perspective in relation to our own person, regarding ourselves no longer with our own eyes but
in the light of God. The humble man no longer
presumes to determine where he stands; he
leaves it to God. The consciousness that God

[18] Rom. 8:32.
[19] Ps. 115:15 (RSV = Ps. 116:15).
[20] Luke 17:10.

attributes importance to him does not evoke
in him a sense of self-importance or a preten-
sion to sovereign autonomy. On the contrary, it
makes him see all the more clearly his weakness,
and the darkness he represents without God and
outside God.

Humility leads us to acknowledge God's personal call

Finally, a third implication of true humility:
our *awareness of God's personal appeal* addressed to each of us as to *this* specified individual. In the prophet Isaiah's words: "I have called
thee by thy name – thou art mine."[21]

There are those who, while they recognize
the glory of God as well as the importance of
man and the call addressed to him in general,
believe, in false humility, that the call is meant
for all others but not for their own person. They
deem their own person too wretched to dare

[21] Isa. 43:1.

assume that they may refer the divine call to themselves. They would hide in a corner and play the part of mere onlookers. The sight of their wretchedness impels them to exclude themselves from the great dialogue between God and man.

This ostensible excess of humility, for all the diffidence it involves, is not free of an element of pride. For here, once more, man presumes to decide himself where he stands, instead of leaving that decision to God. Yet, this is precisely the test of true humility, that one no longer presumes to judge whether or not one is too miserable to be included in the call to sanctity but simply answers the merciful love of God by sinking down in adoration.

The question whether I feel worthy to be called is beside the point; that God *has* called me is the one thing that matters. Having abandoned all pride and all craving for being something of my own resources, I shall not doubt that God, from whom I receive everything,

also has the power to lift me up and to trans-
form any darkness into light: "Thou shalt
wash me, and I shall be made whiter than
snow."[22]

I give up the wish to enlighten God as to
the degree of my worthiness, knowing that by
myself I am worth nothing; but if He wills to
draw me to Him, if He calls me by my name,
my duty is to say the one word: *Adsum* ("Here
I am").[23] Thus did the most humble Virgin
answer the highest call merely by the words:
"Behold the handmaid of the Lord: be it done
to me according to thy word."[24]

The fact that he has been called to a com-
munion with God, that Christ has addressed
His *sequere me* ("follow me") also to him, that
he is one of those to whom He speaks thus,
"Be you therefore perfect, as also your heavenly

[22] Ps. 50:9 (RSV = Ps. 51:7).
[23] Gen. 31:11.
[24] Luke 1:38.

Father is perfect"[25] – this fact, to be sure, must again and again strike man as a manifestation of the inscrutable mercy of God.

He must never take the place which God has assigned him as though it were something evidently due to him; rather he should, on every occasion, begin by saying with St. Peter: "Thou shalt never wash my feet."[26] With trembling heart, he should stand before the Lord in surprise, as it were, and speak with the tongue of the holy Church: "Lord, I am not worthy."

Nevertheless, in all humility, he must *accept* the grace of God. Even though preserving an attitude of wonder and experiencing that grace as something inexplicable, he must yet receive, adding to his "I am not worthy," "but say the word and my soul will be healed."[27]

[25] Matt. 5:48.
[26] John 13:8.
[27] Cf. Matt. 8:8.

Humility contains an element of holy audacity

For to the core of humility belongs a gesture of holy audacity. Just as faith, hope, and charity cannot be without an element of boldness, so also does true humility demand it. Our jubilant assent to our own insignificance, our heroic abandonment of all self-glorification, our relinquishment of self in following Christ – all this is incompatible with tepid mediocrity and cautious smugness.

Humility is the opposite, not only of all *malicious* pride but of all forms of self-centered mediocrity, such as emphasis on petty pleasures or honors, any kind of slavery to conventions, any attachment of importance to unimportant concerns, any cowardice, any bourgeois complacency.

Humility, which springs from our confrontation with God, necessarily bursts the bonds of all mundane immanence, of the peripheral, terrestrial, everyday aspect of all things, based on a vision of the world which would forever bar our access to God. Whereas the virtue of modesty, operating on the level of earthly relationships, is linked to an attitude of quiet reserve or even resignation in which there is no place for boldness, humility implies a heavenward aspiration that carries with it a breath of greatness and holy audacity. The total relinquishment of self, the blissful dying away of the ego – this means an ultimate jubilant freedom; an unthwarted subsistence in truth.

4.

Humility attributes nothing to the self

*H*umility is the antithesis to all forms of pride – above all, to the two types described above, which, for all their distinctness, are both characterized by an act of rebellion against God. But there are other kinds of pride: *self-complacency* and what we may call *haughtiness* or *social pride*. To these, too, humility stands opposed.

Prideful self-complacency uses values to enhance its own position

A person who is merely self-complacent is not blighted with resentment against value as such, nor does he reach out to dethrone values or God, the exemplar of all values. Rather, in order to nourish his consciousness of *counting for much* and his cult of self, he would possess all values. He does not feel insulted by their existence and splendor; he may not even find it difficult to recognize God as the supreme Lord. Rather he would insinuate himself with God and bask in the sunshine of his dignity before God.

At heart, he, too, is afflicted with value-blindness. For it is not the intrinsic importance of the good and the beautiful that moves him; he is interested in values merely as an ornament for his own self. He accepts them as one accepts a convention, out of his desire to stand confirmed and glorious in the face of his fellow men, of himself, and even of God. His pretensions are not so great as those implied in satanic pride. He does not consider challenging values or defying God; his presumption is to use the metaphysical power of values, and the respect they compel, to gratify his pride.

The complacent man does not expressly deny that he has received his grandeur from God: but like the Pharisee of the parable in the Gospel, he boasts of whatever excellence he may possess as though he had it of himself. In his heart of hearts, he fails to take account of the fact that he has received everything from God. The Pharisee, in particular, although not expressly bent on dethroning God, is anxious lest God, as it were, should dethrone *him;* hence, he only tolerates God at a remote distance, a majestic-looking and not very troublesome God whom he may use for the confirmation of his own glory. Against the incarnate God-Man, however, who spells a threat of direct confrontation with God, who is Himself humble and demands humility of others, the Pharisee conceives a mortal hatred.

The quality of self-complacency varies according to the values it abuses

Next, the specific quality of self-complacency varies considerably according to the *class of values* which the subject would abuse for self-decoration. Here we are faced with an apparent paradox. The higher the values of which one boasts, the worse his immorality in doing so. The more the values in question determine an objective elevation and nobility of man, the more reprehensible it is to flaunt them.

Pharisaism

The gravest case, therefore, is that of the Pharisee, who boasts of his piety and of his being "a just man" before the Lord. He would feed his self-infatuation with the highest values, and pass for glorious not merely in the judgment of his fellow men and of himself but in that of God. His motto is "O God, I give Thee thanks that I am not as the rest of men." This type of pride, again, is a specifically malignant one, although not in the same degree as satanic pride. The Pharisee, too, is hardened and incapable of loving kindness and self-surrender.

Self-righteousness

Compared with him, a person who is merely self-righteous in the narrower sense of

the term seems less vicious. Although equal to
the Pharisee in that he, too, advertises his moral
accomplishments, he at least does not abuse the
very highest values — sanctity and justness (in the
Old Testament sense) — but contents himself with
the values of natural morality. He rejoices not in
his stature before God, but in his self-respect
and in the social figure he cuts: the respect he
supposes others pay him.

Men of this kind also take pleasure in con-
templating the defects of others, against which
their own superiority stands out more glow-
ingly. In them, too, there lives an evil resentment, not against value as such, to be sure, but
against the virtues of others, which they experience as a threat to their self-glory.

Although, as has been said, the merely self-
righteous person is by one degree less execrable
than the Pharisee, his attitude is still one of the
prototypes of all morally damnable conduct, and
it insults God. Although Satanism and Pharisaism
proper remain excluded, self-righteousness

makes a person obdurate and void of love to the extent that it takes hold of him.

Lesser forms of self-complacency

Self-complacency centered on intellectual values, however, is incomparably more harmless. A man who glories in his erudition, his acumen, or his genius, a man whose ambition it is to be deemed *remarkable,* presents at any rate a much milder case of moral aberration.

Again, he whose pride is related to his wealth, his title of nobility, or the public honors awarded to him, is tainted with even less malice. The lower a value, the more stupid it is to be conceited on its account and to derive from it a consciousness of counting for much or a feeling of self-glory – the more stupid, but at the same time, the less evil.

This ostensible paradox finds its explanation in the law of ethics stating that the moral evil inherent in the *abuse* of values is directly proportionate to the height of the value.

Why some forms of self-complacency are more harmless than others

Similarly, the less we may claim a value as representing a merit on our part – in other words, the less we, as free beings, are responsible for its possession – the more stupid it will be on our part to exhibit conceit on its score; and the more harmless from a moral point of view will be the pride involved in that conceit. The more we are proud of a value which (as is true of moral values) requires our active participation and effort to be realized, the more reprehensible our pride will be.

This second paradox is accounted for by the fact that our attribution of value to ourselves means a glorification of self in a much stricter and deeper sense whenever the values in question presuppose our free and active – as it were, creative – participation.

Here God has called on us to cooperate with Him; here He has elevated us to the uppermost plane. To abuse this high gift and requite it with a warped response is what makes our pride guilty of a more particular degree of malice.

It must be considered, in addition, that by his pride the Pharisee actually destroys all merit attached to his good works; that is, to put it more explicitly, he lacks the capacity of realizing any moral value so long as he perseveres in his proud attitude. On the other hand, whereas self-complacency does not annihilate intellectual values, it certainly casts an unfavorable light on them insofar as it implies a specific aspect of stupidity. Vital values are still less affected by the fact that they are boasted of, and outward goods – such as wealth or a high social position – least of all.

There is another side to self-complacency which requires mention. This vice involves not merely a self-satisfaction derived from the putative possession of values, but a gnawing ambition to possess them, a restless eagerness to secure them. A kind of dim, smoldering fire seems to consume the souls of such people; they are hardened, shuttered, empty of love; the fury of climbing higher never ceases tormenting them.

Vanity is less harmful than ambitious self-complacency

An attitude widely different from this is *vanity* in the strict sense of the term: the placid, self-sufficient rejoicing in values one presumes oneself to possess. The addict of vanity (in this sense) is not fired by that sinister ambition; he is satisfied with what he has, which he believes to be no small thing. He is not hardened like the self-complacent type previously depicted; rather he displays a trait of pleasure-loving softness.

As contrasted to ambitious self-complacency, vanity represents a comparatively harmless form of pride. A vain person can be good-natured; the ambitiously complacent one, never. More-over, vanity as a rule is referred to intellectual, vital, and exterior assets rather than to religious or moral virtues. What occupies the center of attention here is one's social figure. Nor is it repugnant to the victim of vanity to recognize other people's virtues, if only the particular point to which his vanity refers is not interfered with. Values other than those abused by his vanity do not interest him; he neglects or minimizes them without any note of resentment.

The humble man
attributes nothing to himself

Now, humility embodies a specific antithesis, not only to metaphysical pride, but to all varieties of self-complacency and vanity as well. The humble man is not interested in values as an instrument of decorating his own self and enhancing his dignity; he understands and responds to their importance in themselves. He is interested in the good for its own sake.

He finds the cause of his joy in the *magnalia Dei* – the glory of God as mirrored and signified by the cosmos and its wealth, of values, including, in particular, the values he discerns in human beings other than himself.

Not subject, as we have seen, to the urge of counting for much, he neither boasts of his virtues nor takes pleasure in their contemplation. He knows that he has received whatever good there is in him from God, and attributes nothing to himself. He says with St. Paul, "But God forbid that I should glory, save in the Cross of our Lord Jesus Christ."[28] He does not feel in any way superior to others; even, say, in regard to criminals, his first thought will be, "Who knows what might have become of me, had the grace of God not protected me or had I been exposed to the same temptations?" He considers himself the least among his fellow men, more sinful and unworthy than everyone else.

This does not mean that he should falsify facts and be blind to the defects of others. He need not deny the gifts which God has granted

[28] Gal. 6:14.

to him, nor the fact that he may possess certain advantages in a higher measure than his fellow men. But his attitude in considering his own advantages differs in principle from the one that he takes in reference to other people's perfections.

Degrees of awareness of our own perfections

In our awareness of our own perfections, three degrees can be distinguished. First, our mere consciousness or knowledge of them, registering them as plain facts. Next – and here begins perversion – the pleasure we take in them. This implies a behavior on man's part as though he possessed those virtues by himself and in his own right, even though theoretically he may not deny that he owes them to God. He anticipates a favorable judgment, a confirmation of his worth, which is ultimately reserved to God alone, and in an analogical sense to his fellow men, but on no account to himself.

While glorying in or boasting of one's advantages is *a fortiori* incompatible with humility, their pleasurable contemplation – as has been shown – is also an offspring of pride; for what vanity delights in is not the value as such but its ornamental function in the service of the ego. Accordingly, a vain person is indifferent to values exhibited by others, and interested only in those which he deems to be distinctive of himself.

But, so one might object, why should it be wrong of man to delight in his own values, even in the sense of taking delight in objective value? Why should he be encouraged to discover, to recognize, and to rejoice in the values of others, and at the same time be bidden to forego any such rejoicing in his own virtues, nay, to suppress in his mind any emphatic awareness of them?

Humility proscribes all contemplation of one's own virtues

It is here that we reach the core of humility, its innermost secret, as it were. In addition to banning all desire to count for much, all proud glorying and all vain delighting in one's own self, humility, indeed, proscribes all contemplation of one's own values, nor does it even tolerate any keen consciousness of them.

The reason is, first, that humility implies our consciousness of our own frailty and of the constant danger of sin in which we live, and above all, a trembling anxiety lest we should lapse into pride. No one is truly humble unless he is imbued with the sense of the permanent menace which pride represents to fallen man. As the Psalmist says, "Set a watch, O Lord, before my mouth: and a door round about my lips. Incline not my heart to evil words; to make excuses in sins."[29]

Because the terrible sin of pride, which he repudiates with all his heart, is always present to his eyes, the humble man will never direct his glance to any one of his virtues, lest he should

[29] Ps. 140:3-4 (RSV = Ps. 141:3-4).

lapse into pride and (in however disguised a fashion) attribute that virtue to a primary goodness of his own self. In holy modesty he will extend a veil over any values discernible in him and never seek to reveal the ultimate value hidden in the depth of his being.

To be sure, he has to know about the abilities with which God has equipped him, if only to be aware of the responsibility they entail. Yet, these abilities must appear to him in the light of the tasks they impose on him, rather than as values which he owns. Having regard to the responsibility he is charged with, linked to his consciousness of being *an unprofitable servant,* he will not abandon himself to the enjoyment of "his" values. Nor will he, lastly, yield to the suasion of that false sense of security which suggests that he might, without lapsing into pride, consider his advantages and enjoy them in a pure response to value as though they were the virtues of another. For *the false sense of security is itself an offspring of pride.*

Humility

Contemplation of our own
virtues eviscerates them

Moreover, the ethical and religious values of
the person himself, as constituted by and founded
upon his response to the value (of a good), are
essentially outside his field of vision. Because
they are built up by the person's response to
value, they do not themselves enter his consciousness in his experience of the values which
elicit his response. The self-values thus displayed
remain, as it were, on the margin of his consciousness; their presence is but indirectly mani-
fested by the interior peace and luminous
harmony that brighten his soul in the act of re-
sponding to the values whose call he experiences.

When our glance alights upon the ethical value
of our moral action or value-response *itself*, we
lose contact with the value *referred* to in that act
or response; and with that contact disappears
the ethical value of our attitude: the more we
admire it, the more thoroughly it disappears.

Hence, it is strictly impossible in the same act to refer our value-response to the value of our own response in a given case. Even with respect to our own attitudes in the past, it is impossible to look at their value and to take delight in them.

It is not impossible to display an ethically valuable behavior and later to reflect upon it with satisfaction; yet even this is destructive of value and inconsistent with humility. For it still severs our contact with the value to which our original moral attitude, the object of our subsequent contemplation, was referred and devoted; it therefore undermines our moral continuity with the subject of our past action, reducing the memory of our accomplishment to an empty shell whose content of value has evaporated.

The humble man is ever conscious of his own imperfections

More than that, far from relishing or even pondering over his own values, the truly humble person is likely to look upon himself, after the example of many saints, as the greatest sinner. For he is most keenly aware of the gratuitousness of the grace he has received; and the higher he has risen objectively, the more clearly he sees the abyss that separates him from the infinite holiness of God. He measures his station, not by what he represents absolutely, but by the distance between what he has received from God and what he has actually accomplished. It is inherent in ethical perfection to be constantly advancing toward Christ and never to attribute to one's moral status a completeness which would give one the feeling of being the possessor of a value.

Humility does not prevent a person from seeing that, with God's help, he has been making progress in some direction; but he must never lose sight of the essential relativity of that progress. The determination never to cease advancing – a process that has no end in this life – is one of the basic conditions of holiness.

Humility attributes nothing to the self

To sum up: we must not indulge in a contemplation of our own values; much less can
we enjoy them even in the sense of a response
to value. Our position in relation to ourselves is
intrinsically different from what it is in relation
to others. Accordingly, too, love of self is not
love in the full and proper sense of the term,
as is the one typified by our love for another
person. Self-love is confined to our concern for
our own happiness and salvation, together with
our assent to the divine idea of a fully deployed
value-response which we are ordained to realize; it lacks those aspects of delight in the beauty
and in the splendor of values which are proper
to our love of other persons.

This fundamental difference between our
position toward ourselves and toward other
persons is also revealed in humility. We are to
lift our eyes to the majestic splendor of God
and to God's reflection in our fellow men.

As regards our relation with ourselves,
however, we are to look at our defects and the

77

vastness which separates us from the glory of
God; the talents and the gifts of grace which
God has given to us we are to consider only
insofar as is necessary in order to examine what
use we have made of them. Walking in the
paths of God, a life pleasing to God will suffuse
our consciousness, as said above, with the inward happiness and peace evoked by the soul's
concord with the world of values; whereas it
would but undo its own meaning and disprove
its own truth, were it to seduce us into an ap-
preciative contemplation of "our" values. Others
may do that, never we ourselves.

**Haughtiness prizes independence
and self-assertion**

We have, lastly, to speak of a further and distinct form of pride, which may be described as
haughtiness or social pride.[30] *Haughtiness* refers,

[30] The French term is *fierté,* in contradistinction to
orgueil, meaning pride in the general and theological
sense; the German terms *Stolz* and *Hochmut* are

not to a perverse attitude to value, but to a re-
pugnance against submission to other persons.
It may not hinder a man from giving a positive
response to impersonal values or from comply-
ing with a demand of morality. But the haughty
man will find it intolerable to feel dependent on
other persons, to serve others, to subordinate
himself to an alien will, and above all, to suffer
ever so slight a humiliation. He is unable to admit before others of having been in the wrong,
even if he knows it in his heart; much less could
he prevail on himself to ask anybody's forgive-
ness. He is stricken with a crabbed anxiousness
about preserving his dignity, which mostly takes
the form of preoccupation concerning his rights
and his honor.

In his relations with others, he lays great
stress on occupying the stronger position. He
frequently declines the voluntary help of others,

respectively equivalent to these, notwithstanding
the etymological kinship between *Hochmut* and
haughty.

lest its acceptance should be construed as an avowal of weakness. He is loath to engage in any partnership where his would not be the senior position. He is eminently hard and inclined to despise compassion as a sign of feebleness.

Haughty men are for the most part fanatics of the idol of "manliness." Neither a resentment against value as such nor the abuse of values as an ornament for the ego belongs to their characteristic defects. All their interests subserve their urge for *self-assertion*. They may not grudge recognition of another's merits, but are highly reluctant to perform any act of obedience, to endure any kind of slight, to yield or to surrender in any fashion.

It is for this reason that the haughty man, even though admitting in his conscience that he has done wrong and regretting his conduct, is incapable of genuine repentance. Much less would he admit his wrong to others and make amends. Confession and the very spirit of the

Confiteor[31] are therefore essentially distasteful
to him.

Haughtiness exists in various degrees

Haughtiness can attain various degrees. It
may go so far as to interfere with man's subordination to God, whenever this demand assumes
a concrete form which appears too painful to
bear. There is a type of haughty person who
would not bend his knees even before God.

As a rule, however, the vice of haughtiness
only affects man's relations with his fellow
men. What the haughty person is chiefly bent
upon is to avoid receiving anything as a gift
from others, accepting any mercy or sympathy,
being in the debt of anyone else, or owing gratitude to anyone. Every act that would imply on
his part a recognition of any kind of dependence on others is connected, in his feeling, with

---

[31] "I confess": the prayer used in the penitential rite
in the Liturgy.

an unbearable loss of dignity. For instance, although he may not find it difficult to acknowl-
edge other people's merits of his own accord,
he would at once feel it incompatible with his
dignity to do so, were he to suspect that his
homage was counted upon as an obligatory
tribute.

Again, while he may be willing to respect
official prerogatives or codified laws, he will
meticulously refuse every gesture of submission
to any authority not strictly official or legal in
character. The haughty person, in a word, is
hard, cramped, and morally close-fisted. His
behavior constitutes an express antithesis to
charity, loving kindness, and readiness to serve;
it forms the utmost contrast to a soul penetrated
and opened up by the light of Jesus.

This form of pride, too, is evil and entirely incompatible with our transformation in Christ.[32]

---

[32] See Dietrich von Hildebrand, *Transformation in
Christ* (Manchester, New Hampshire: Sophia
Institute Press, 1990).

The pride of the stoic or the cynic is of this kind.
And it is this pride which is erected into an ideal
at war with charity and humility, in the famous
lines of Horace: "If the world should collapse
in ruins about him, struck by its fragments he
would remain fearless."[33] It is the same pride
which is at the basis of many a form of fearless-
ness and *natural virility*. There is nothing the
haughty soul dreads so much as fear. Yet, it is
precisely he who so often becomes a slave to
the basest kind of fear – the fear of other people's judgment, which is also called *human
respect*. (This mad pursuer of independence is
very dependent on the admiration others give
to his independence.)

This type of man, then, is loath to ask for
anything and convinced that he is above the
need of redemption. He abhors any situation
in which the goodwill of others (or its absence)
would affect him; he is infatuated with the

[33] *Odes,* Bk. 3, no. 3, l. 7.

idol of his "upright" self-sufficiency; and he is
ashamed of any movement of love or compassion, indeed of any kind of sentiment. In a
word, he is an epitome of cramped tension.
Humility embodies an integral negation of this
type of man.

Humility does not fear legitimate subordination to others

He in whom humility is present does not
have to overcome any inner resistance in order
to subordinate himself to others. In his supple
freedom of soul, he always keeps aware of basic
realities and is past seeking freedom in the im-
mature illusion of self-sufficiency. As long as it
does not interfere with his devotion and obedience to God, his dependence on other men by
no means evokes in him a sense of oppression.
He receives the breath of mercy with gratitude.
The consciousness of being in someone's debt
does not distress him at all; the thought of being
the weaker partner in relation to another does

not disturb the peace of his soul. Nor does it embarrass him to have to ask someone's pardon or to confess a wrong he has done. For he is free of all spasm of autarchy and of all allegiance to the idol of stoic virility. Even at the social level, he preserves Christian indifference to self; he wills to be nothing and to count for nothing. All this, however, derives its character of true humility from the subject's *attitude toward* God.

Humility is neither spinelessness nor servility

For humility proper is not the only possible antithesis to social pride: there are others of a purely natural (and some of them of a morally negative) character. Such is, for example, the spineless, pliant type of man, whom one may treat as one likes, who suffers any insult or humiliation without defending himself, not because in his freedom of soul he has rid himself of all pride and egotism, but because he is too spiritless and feeble to think of resistance or too cowardly to risk any conflict.

Another form of the absence of social pride that must not be confused with humility is the one which denotes the specifically servile nature. This type of man cannot live except as a hanger-on, a subordinate to some strong and powerful personality. Dependence on others means to him no discomfort at all; the position of a lackey or flunky is what suits his inclinations. Being a satellite is natural to him and the sole condition in which he feels happy.

At the same time, he is by no means necessarily free from pride. In given circumstances, he may ride roughshod over weaker ones or social inferiors. He is very sensitive to honors and greedy of praise for his services; his natural submissiveness, the expression of his constitutional need of leaning on a stronger personality, has nothing to do with that relinquishment of self which issues from our confrontation with God.

Apart from these morally negative contrasts to haughtiness, there are yet even further natural varieties of the capacity for self-subordination, which may impress us favorably rather than otherwise, but must still be distinguished from humility. Thus, the disposition we find in many women to center their lives in full self-surrender to serving a man and supplementing his personality, to seek support in him in a way comparable to the ivy clinging to a tree; or again, the modesty prompting a man to keep demurely to an inferior station, instead of affecting the first place in the manner of the haughty. These attitudes, too, are the fruits of a natural need or a certain reasonable sobriety – they are not humility.

Humility originates in the right response to God

For, even in the perspective of our relations with our fellow men, true humility has its origin in our *right response to God*, which implies not only our awareness of the glory and omnipotence of God, and of our own creaturely finiteness, but a total emancipation from our spasm of self-centeredness in the presence of Christ. He is humble in whose heart the infinite merciful love of God, which bends down to us in the person of Christ – the descent of God, who longs to gather the lost sheep, and who solicits our love – has dissolved all pride, even the hidden and the limited one, and has reduced all self-assertion: that is what places him in an entirely new position even in regard to his fellow men.

In its full and specific unfolding, humility calls forth what we can describe as the virtue of meekness.[34] The humble one has divested himself of all hardness; he faces his fellow men, not mailed and armored, but in the luminous attire of invincible charity. Even his foes – and

---

[34] See von Hildebrand, *Transformation in Christ,* ch. 14.

this is the test of meekness – he confronts unarmed.

In specific contradistinction to the haughty character, the humble man is not hampered by any inhibitions in subordinating himself to others; he is past all self-assertion and therefore ready to obey all authority that has its place in the divine plan. He sets himself at a distance from his own arbitrary will and does not seek satisfaction in the consciousness of unbridled freedom. Whereas a haughty person (apart from the question of the particular objects for which he strives) resents and feels any curb placed on his arbitrary good pleasure to be intolerable, the person imbued with humility adopts as his maxim – in conformity with the seventh chapter of St. Benedict's Rule – the words of our Lord: "I am not come to do my will, but the will of Him who hath sent me."[35] Likewise St. Benedict says, concerning the third stage of humility:

[35] John 6:38.

Humility

"Out of his love of God, the monk submits himself to his superior in perfect obedience." *Holy obedience,* the expression of a complete breach with self-will and self-assertion, is that actualization of humility which is most explicitly opposed to social pride.

Christian humility calls us to acts of self-humiliation

But we must go one step further. He whose soul has become a seat of consummate humility is not only able to confess his wrongs with ease, to submit himself or to bear an offense with resignation; he actually *elects to be the last.* He yearns for the practice of obedience; he is glad to suffer slights and is avid for contempt and rebuke. It is here that we reach the mysterious innermost core of Christian humility.

What the latter implies is not merely a liberation from pride in its various forms (including haughtiness); not merely a recognition of our true metaphysical situation and an emergence

90

from all illusions; not merely the habit of seeing ourselves in blissful freedom of soul as we appear in the eyes of God and of giving our joyous assent to this truth.

Beyond that, Christian humility implies an express act of *self-humiliation,* a voluntary descent *beneath* our legitimate natural dignity, an act of reducing ourselves to naught before God. It implies the gesture of a permanent inner dying of the self, in order that Christ may live in us – a gesture that has found its unique expression in the figure of St. John the Baptist and in his words: "He must increase, but I must decrease."[36]

If, as has been pointed out earlier, humility is only conceivable as a response to the personal God of Christian revelation, again, this deepest fulfillment of humility is only conceivable as a response to the God-Man, Jesus Christ; to the very gesture of descent performed by Him who

[36]John 3:30.

"emptied Himself, taking the form of a servant, being made in the likeness of men and in habit found as a man; humbled Himself, becoming obedient unto death, even to the death of the cross."[37]

Let us represent to ourselves the ineffable scene, as reported by St. John in his Gospel: "When supper was done (the devil having now put into the heart of Judas Iscariot, the son of Simon, to betray Him), knowing that the Father had given Him all things into His hands and that He came from God and goeth to God, He riseth from supper and, having taken a towel, girded Himself. After that, He putteth water into a basin and began to wash the feet of the disciples and to wipe them with the towel wherewith He was girded. . . . Then after He had washed their feet and taken His garments, being set down again, He said to them: 'Know you what I have done to you? You call me

[37] Phil. 2:7-8.

Master and Lord. And you say well: for so I
am. If then I, being your Lord and Master,
have washed your feet, you also ought to
wash one another's feet. For I have given you
an example, that as I have done to you, so you
do also.' "[38]

Thus does Christ call on us to step down
from the natural position in which God has
installed us. *Humility* certainly means the habit
of living in the truth. Beyond that, however, it
means an active gesture of quitting the status
that is our natural due – a step toward reducing
ourselves to naught. It constitutes a specific
element in the imitation of Christ.

Here the deep connection between humility
and charity manifests itself. In its deepest roots,
humility is a fruit of charity; it is our love of
Christ that makes us will to "die" so that He
may live in us and inspires our readiness to
serve all men, because He has said: "What you

[38] John 13:2-15.

do to the least of my brethren, you have done it to me."[39]

Such alone as have absorbed the spirit of these words of the Lord: "Even as the Son of man is not come to be ministered unto, but to minister"[40] – such hearts alone as have been wounded to the core by this descent of love "unto the end,"[41] may acquire the humility that has filled the saints; the humility that made every insult, every injustice, every humiliation taste sweet to them; that caused them permanently to undergo the process of self-surrender and self-humiliation, and stirred up in their souls the fire of an unlimited readiness to serve.

Christian humility proper encloses the mystery of an inward descent down to the abyss of nothingness, so that God may be "all in all"[42] within us.

[39] Matt. 25:40.
[40] Matt. 20:28.
[41] John 13:1.
[42] Eph. 1:23.

Humility confers beauty
on the humble soul

He who lives in humility deliberately assigns to himself a place even beneath the one which he can naturally claim. He is like the guest to whom the Lord has said, "Friend, rise higher."[43] Humility, therefore, is not only a presupposition for the genuineness and truth of all our virtues, but is the central condition of our transformation and regeneration in Christ. Moreover, it embodies a high value in itself, conferring on man a unique kind of beauty.

Humility bursts the bonds of all narrowness; through it, even a personality insignificant by nature will acquire width and greatness. For it is only the humble soul, the soul that has emptied itself, which can be fully penetrated by the divine Life it has received in holy Baptism; and it is upon such a soul that there falls a reflection

[43]Luke 14:10.

of the greatness and infinitude of God. Here is a great mystery, paradoxical yet true: precisely he who speaks the word of total assent to his finiteness and *limitation* will thereby illuminate his nature with an aura which in some way images the *unlimited* breadth of God. In him alone who *dies* inwardly, descending almost beneath the natural level of being that has been his due in the order of creation, who wills no longer to occupy any *space* at all, may the wealth of supernatural life blossom out, according to St. Paul's words: "I live, yet it is not I who live but Christ who lives in me."[44]

"Everyone that exalteth himself shall be humbled; and he that humbleth himself shall be exalted."[45] The exaltation of the humble is by no means merely a reward which God grants to them in life eternal; it is also an intrinsic effect of humility, accomplished even on earth. For

[44]Gal. 2:20.
[45]Luke 14:11.

indeed, the humble walk as if clad in the attire of a unique nobility, before which all splendor of purely natural talents and gifts wanes into insignificance. By his descent beneath his natural rank, the humble man in a mystical sense prostrates himself, at the feet of the Lord, as did St. Mary Magdalene.[46] He is lifted up by Jesus and thus enters the celestial realm.

All height, width, and depth, all greatness and beauty of humility, with its irresistible victorious power, shine forth most luminously in the Blessed Virgin, the Queen of the angels and all saints. In humility there is mirrored the central mystery of the process of our transformation – the mystery that our Lord has put into these words: "Unless the grain of wheat falling into the ground die, itself remaineth alone; but if it die, it bringeth forth much fruit."[47] The path that leads man to his ultimate union with Christ is

[46]Luke 10:39; John 11:32; John 12:3.
[47]John 12:24-25 (RSV = John 12:24).

not the unfolding of his natural powers and of the wealth of his gifts but his radical renunciation of self-assertion, the relinquishment and mortification of the self. "He who loses his soul shall win it."[48]

Thus, yearning to be transformed in Christ, we must pray: *Jesus, meek and humble of heart, make our hearts like unto Thine.*

[48] Cf. Mark 8:35; Luke 9:24.

About this book

Humility is an excerpt from Dietrich von Hildebrand's spiritual masterpiece, *Transformation in Christ,* which he wrote during his heroic – and nearly fatal – struggle against the Nazis (see biographical note). In this classic, von Hildebrand shows why answering God's call to holiness means that we must be *transformed into Christ, a*nd he explains the virtues for which we must strive in order to undergo this transformation.

Transformation in Christ examines in detail each of the following essentials for holiness: readiness to change, contrition, self-knowledge, consciousness, simplicity, recollection and contemplation, humility, confidence, striving for perfection, freedom, hunger for justice, patience, love of peace, meekness, mercy, holy sorrow, sobriety, and surrender of self.

Humility

Often likened to *The Imitation of Christ*
by those who have praised its extraordinary
spiritual wisdom, *Transformation in Christ* will
help you recognize and overcome your frailties
and fears as you discover your own path to
holiness.

Transformation in Christ is published by
Sophia Institute Press. For information on
ordering, see the last page of this book.

Biographical note

Dietrich von Hildebrand (1889-1977)

*H*itler feared him, and the late Pope Pius XII called him "the twentieth-century Doctor of the Church." For more than six decades, Dietrich von Hildebrand – philosopher, spiritual writer, and anti-Nazi crusader – led philosophical, religious, and political groups, lectured throughout Europe and the Americas, and published more than thirty books and many more articles. His influence was widespread and endures to this day.

Although von Hildebrand was a deep and original thinker on subjects ranging across the spectrum of human interests, nonetheless, in his lectures and writings, he instinctively avoided extravagant speculations and convoluted theories. Instead, he sought to illuminate the nature and significance of seemingly "everyday" elements of human existence that are easily misunderstood and too frequently taken for granted. Therefore, much of von Hildebrand's philosophy concerns the human person, the person's interior ethical and affective life, and the relations that should exist between the person and the world in which he finds himself.

Von Hildebrand's background made him uniquely qualified to examine these topics. He was born in beautiful Florence in 1889, the son of the renowned German sculptor Adolf von Hildebrand. At the time, the von Hildebrand home was a center of art and culture, visited by the greatest European artists and musicians of the day. Young Dietrich's early acquaintance with these vibrant, creative people intensified his natural zest for life.

In Florence, von Hildebrand was surrounded by beauty – the overwhelming natural beauty of the Florentine countryside and the rich beauty of the many art treasures that are Florence's Renaissance heritage. Pervading this Florentine atmosphere was Catholicism: in the art, in the architecture, and in the daily life of the people. These early years in Florence quickened in von Hildebrand a passionate love of truth, of goodness, of beauty, and of Christianity.

As he grew older, he developed a deep love for philosophy, studying under some of the greatest of the early twentieth-century German philosophers, including Edmund Husserl, Max Scheler, and Adolf Reinach. Converting to Catholicism in 1914, von Hildebrand taught philosophy for many years at the University of Munich.

However, soon after the end of World War I, Nazism began to threaten von Hildebrand's beloved southern Germany. With his characteristic clear-sightedness, von Hildebrand immediately discerned its intrinsic evil. From its earliest days, he vociferously denounced Nazism in articles and speeches throughout Germany and the rest of Europe.

Declaring himself unwilling to continue living in a country ruled by a criminal, von Hildebrand regretfully left his native Germany for Austria, where he continued teaching philosophy (now at the University of Vienna) and fought the Nazis with even greater vigor, founding and then publishing for a number of years a prominent anti-Nazi newspaper, *Christliche Ständestaat.*

This angered both Heinrich Himmler and Adolf Hitler, who were determined to silence von Hildebrand and close his anti-Nazi newspaper. Orders were given to have von Hildebrand assassinated in Austria. However, he evaded the hit-squads and, thanks to his Swiss passport, was able to flee the country just as it fell to the Nazis.

It is characteristic of von Hildebrand that even while he was engaged in this dangerous life-and-death struggle against the Nazis, he maintained his deep spiritual life, and managed to write during this period his greatest work, the sublime and highly acclaimed spiritual classic *Transformation in Christ,* from which *Humility* is taken.

Biographical note

Fleeing from Austria, von Hildebrand was pursued through many countries, ultimately arriving on the shores of America in 1940 by way of France, Spain, Portugal, and Brazil.

Penniless in New York after his heroic struggle against the Nazis, von Hildebrand was hired as professor of philosophy at Fordham University where he taught until his retirement. Many of his best works were written during this period and after his retirement. He died in 1977 in New Rochelle, New York.

Dietrich von Hildebrand was remarkable for his keen intellect, his profound originality, his prodigious output, his great personal courage, his deep spirituality, and his intense love of truth, goodness, and beauty. These rare qualities made him one of the greatest philosophers and one of the wisest men of the twentieth century.

*S*ophia

*I*nstitute

*P*ress®

Sophia Institute is a nonprofit institution that seeks to restore man's knowledge of eternal truth, including man's knowledge of his own nature, his relation to other persons, and his relation to God.

Sophia Institute Press® publishes translations of foreign works to make them accessible for the first time to English-speaking readers, brings back into print books that have been long out of print, and publishes important new books that fulfill the ideals of Sophia Institute. These books afford readers a rich source of the enduring wisdom of mankind.

Sophia Institute Press® makes these high-quality books available to the public by using advanced technology and by soliciting donations to subsidize its general publishing costs. Your generosity can help provide the public with editions of works containing the enduring wisdom of the ages. Please send your tax-deductible contribution to the address below.

For your free catalog,
call toll-free:
1-800-888-9344

or write:
Sophia Institute Press®
Box 5284
Manchester, NH 03108

website: http:\\www.sophiainstitute.com

Sophia Institute is a tax-exempt institution
as defined by the Internal Revenue Code,
Section 501(c)(3). Tax I.D. 22-2548708.